GODS
-AND-
MONSTERS

THE MYTHS AND LEGENDS OF ANCIENT WORLDS

Stella Caldwell

My job as an archaeologist takes me around the world. I have spent long weeks digging for desert artifacts, and exploring the icy landscapes of northern lands. As a diver, I have seen the mysterious ruins of sunken cities, and have scoured riverbeds to uncover long-held secrets.

Several years ago, I took part in a dig on Mount Lykaion in Greece. This was the mythical birthplace of Zeus, the ancient Greek god of the sky. Among our finds was a small statue of the god, which seemed to exude a heavenly power.

The statue of Zeus reminded me of an artifact I stumbled upon a few years earlier in Rome—a coin which had the head of the god Jupiter on one side. Jupiter was the Roman god of the sky.

A few months later I was invited to join a dig on Greenland, the remote island colonized by the Vikings around 1,000 years ago. Among the artifacts unearthed was a silver Thor's hammer pendant. Thor was the Norse god of thunder, and his magical hammer defended both gods and humans from harm.

Some time later I volunteered to join divers exploring the lost city of Thonis-Heracleion, submerged beneath the sea some 1,200 years ago. Wonderful treasures such as giant statues and ships have been discovered there. It was no surprise that my first find was an Eye of Horus amulet—the all-seeing eye of the Egyptian sky god and a powerful symbol of protection.

My tale is a strange one, but it has made me consider the connections between different mythologies. The objects discovered on my explorations are displayed in this book.
This is a story of powerful gods, brave heroes, and terrifying beasts of long-ago worlds.

Stella Caldwell,
London

THE GREEKS AND ROMANS

Greek and Roman myths tell of powerful gods and goddesses, of mysterious spirits and nymphs, and of fearless heroes that conquered terrifying monsters. These ancient tales, passed from one generation to the next, and mirrored in artifacts buried in ancient ruins, are some of the greatest stories ever told . . .

THE ANCIENT GREEKS

Thousands of years ago, the ancient Greeks developed a way of life that was to shape western civilization. They introduced important ideas in politics, science, and philosophy, and excelled in arts and sports. As a way of understanding the world, the Greeks told each other extraordinary tales of gods, heroes, and monsters.

This gold death mask was found in a royal grave at Mycenae.

An ancient Greek coin dating from the fifth century BC. It shows the goddess Athena.

The First Greeks

The Minoan civilization flourished on the island of Crete, roughly between 2700 and 1500 BC. The people here lived in large settlements based around rich palaces. After the fall of the Minoans, the peoples of Mycenae dominated the Greek world until around 1200 BC. The Mycenaeans were warriors and traders, and traveled far and wide.

The Golden Age of Athens

From the eighth century BC, independent settlements known as city-states, such as Sparta and Athens, grew up on the Greek mainland, and colonies were created overseas. By the fifth century BC, Athens was a magnificent center of culture and learning.

The Parthenon, a temple built for the goddess Athena, still stands on a rocky hill called the Acropolis in Athens.

A Roman mosaic showing Alexander the Great.

The End of an Era

In 336 BC, Alexander the Great became the ruler of the Greek kingdom of Macedonia. He led a huge army and created an empire stretching all the way to India. After Alexander's death, this empire was divided into four Greek-ruled kingdoms. By 30 BC, however, all of Greece had fallen to the rising power of the Romans.

WARFARE

War was an everyday part of ancient Greek life, and the country's myths are full of battles. The Trojan War is the most famous war in Greek mythology. Other myths tell of a fearsome race of female warriors called the Amazons, who were considered to be the physical equals of men.

A Spartan warrior's helmet.

GODS AND GODDESSES

High on the peaks of Mount Olympus lived immortal Zeus and the other Olympian gods. Although human in form and with many flaws, these powerful gods reigned supreme over the universe. There were a host of lesser gods, too.

Apollo, god of truth and prophecy.

Artemis, goddess of hunting.

THE TITANS

Before the Olympians, the mighty Titans ruled the universe. Their ruler, Cronus, and his wife, Rhea, had many children. To avoid being overthrown by his offspring, Cronus swallowed each newborn god. However, when Zeus was born, Rhea hid the child away and tricked her husband into swallowing a boulder instead. When Zeus had grown up, he punched his father in the stomach to make him vomit up the other gods, and led them in a terrible war against the Titans. Zeus was victorious and Cronus was eventually banished from Earth.

Dionysus was the god of wine and celebration.

Hestia was the goddess of the home and family.

Demeter was the goddess of fertility and harvest.

Hades was the lord of the underworld.

The Olympians

All the gods had their own areas of influence. Zeus was lord of the sky, while Poseidon was ruler of the seas, and Ares was the god of war. Aphrodite was the beautiful goddess of love and Athena the goddess of wisdom. The Greeks believed Apollo, the god of truth and prophecy, could foretell the future, while his twin sister, Artemis, was the goddess of hunting.

Ruler of the Dead

Although he was not an Olympian, Hades, the lord of the underworld and ruler of the dead, was an important god. Cerberus, a ferocious three-headed hound, guarded the entrance to Hades' dark kingdom. All dead souls were permitted to enter—but none could ever leave.

ZEUS, KING OF THE GODS

Zeus was the supreme god of ancient Greece. He was also the god of the sky, shaping the weather according to his temper. He stood in judgment over gods and mortals. Those who angered him could expect to be struck down by a thunderbolt, or condemned to the dark underworld Tartarus.

THE EAGLE OF ZEUS

A golden eagle served as Zeus's messenger, appearing at his side. One myth tells of how the eagle was once a virtuous king named Periphas. When the king came to be honored as a god, Zeus was furious and would have struck him down with a thunderbolt. However, the god Apollo quickly transformed Periphas into an eagle, setting him down by the throne of Zeus. The god's other symbols were a thunderbolt and scepter.

Zeus and Hera on Mount Olympus, the home of the gods.

Hera's Revenge

Zeus was married to his sister, Hera, the goddess of marriage and childbirth. The marriage was not happy, and Hera was often jealous of her husband's many love affairs. One myth tells of how Zeus fell for a pretty river nymph called Io. When Hera discovered the romance, Zeus transformed the nymph into a small white cow.

But Hera was not fooled and asked for the cow as a gift. The goddess instructed a hundred-eyed giant to guard Io, but Zeus helped her to escape. When Hera found out, she sent a horsefly to sting and torment the cow Io as she wandered the world forever without rest.

There is a strange energy that seems to flow from this little statue of Zeus as if the god were still living ...

Stella Caldwell

POSEIDON

As the king of the oceans, Poseidon had the power to stir the sea to a fury or to calm raging waters with a glance. Seafaring was an important part of Greek life, and sailors and fishermen prayed to Poseidon for protection. However, this Olympian was also a vengeful god, and he was often referred to as the "Earth-shaker." When angered, Poseidon punished mortals with devastating earthquakes.

HEROES AND DEMIGODS

The heroes of mythical Greece possessed great strength and performed incredible feats of bravery. Some, like Jason, the legendary leader of the Argonauts, were mortals. Others, such as Zeus's son, Perseus, had one divine parent and were demigods.

Jason holds the golden fleece in this statue from Rome, Italy.

Jason and the Golden Fleece

Jason wanted to reclaim the kingdom of Iolcos from his wicked uncle, Pelias. However, Pelias told him he must first fetch the Golden Fleece–the pelt of a magical ram guarded by a dragon–from Colchis. With a band of heroes called the Argonauts, Jason sailed for Colchis in a ship named the *Argo*.

The Golden Fleece hung from the branch of a sacred oak tree. As Jason approached it, he heard the dragon's terrifying hiss. A sorceress named Medea had given Jason a sleeping potion to sprinkle over the beast. When it had fallen asleep, Jason seized his prize and sped back to the waiting ship.

This famous portrayal of Medusa is by famous artist Michelangelo Merisi da Caravaggio.

Perseus and Medusa

King Polydectes of Seriphos once fell in love with a beautiful woman called Danae. However, her son, Perseus, despised him. Polydectes longed to get rid of Perseus so he sent him on a quest to fetch Medusa's head. This snake-haired monster was one of three deadly sisters called the Gorgons—a single glance at their hideous faces would turn anyone to stone.

An enormous dragon guarded the Golden Fleece at all times.

Athena gave Perseus a shield and Hermes gave him winged sandals, a sword, and a helmet that would make him invisible. The hero flew to the Gorgons' lair, where Medusa slept. As he crept closer, Medusa awoke and turned her terrible stare upon him. Perseus avoided her gaze by looking only at her reflection on his shield. Drawing his sword, he sliced off her head.

Perseus holds up Medusa's severed head in this bronze statue in Florence, Italy.

HERACLES

Heracles was the son of the god Zeus and a mortal called Alcmene. Zeus's wife, Hera, was furious that her husband had fathered a demigod, and she cast a spell on Heracles that caused him to murder his wife and children. King Eurystheus set Heracles 12 "impossible" tasks in order to make up for his terrible crime.

Slaying the Nemean Lion

To kill the savage Nemean lion whose sharp claws could cut through armor was Heracles's first "labor." Armed with a club, bow and arrow, and a sword, Heracles searched for the lion. He heard a terrible roar and suddenly the beast was upon him. Heracles released an arrow but it was useless against the creature.

Wrapping his powerful arms around the lion, the hero now relied on his incredible strength to strangle it. Heracles then used one of the lion's lethal claws to remove the creature's skin and made himself an impenetrable cloak.

Taking Cerberus

The final and most dangerous task for Heracles was to kidnap Cerberus, the ferocious hound of the underworld. Few mortals had ever descended to the land of the dead, and Cerberus permitted nobody to leave. Hades, the king of the underworld, agreed to let Heracles borrow his hound as long as the hero could overpower him with nothing but brute strength.

As Heracles approached Cerberus, he heard the beast's spine-chilling barks. The hero grasped the creature's three savage heads and wrestled him into submission. Heracles then tied a chain to the whimpering Cerberus and led him up from the darkness.

A Roman carving showing Heracles leading the chained hound Cerberus.

Heracles wrestles with the Nemean lion.

Heracles was strong even as a baby. He killed two snakes that Hera sent to kill him.

FABULOUS CREATURES

Pegasus was tamed by the hero Bellerophon.

Ancient Greece teemed with fearsome beasts, from deadly dragons and serpents to the one-eyed giants called Cyclops. Some creatures were made up of different animals, like the majestic winged griffin. Others, such as the vulture-like harpies or the man-eating Sphinx, were part human, part animal.

Most centaurs were aggressive creatures, known for their wild behavior.

Half Man, Half Beast

Centaurs were part man, part horse, and most were known for their savage behavior. The Theban Sphinx had the head of a woman, the body of a lion, the wings of an eagle, and a serpent's tail. She devoured anyone who couldn't answer her riddle–although when the hero Oedipus finally guessed the correct answer, the Sphinx flung herself from a cliff.

The Winged Stallion

Pegasus was a winged stallion that sprang from the blood of Medusa when Perseus cut off her head. It was with the help of Pegasus that the hero Bellerophon was able to slay the fire-breathing monster known as the Chimera. The Chimera had a lion's head, a goat's head rising from its back, and a serpent's head at the end of its tail.

TYPHON

Known as the "father of all monsters," the hundred-headed dragon Typhon rose up to challenge Zeus after his defeat of the Titans. The god imprisoned the dragon under Mount Etna, a volcano on the island of Sicily. Legend has it that whenever the trapped beast writhes in rage, Mount Etna boils and spits out columns of fire.

THESEUS AND THE MINOTAUR

Theseus was a hero of ancient Athens who once battled with the ferocious Minotaur. This fearsome beast was half man and half bull. Imprisoned in a huge maze called the Labyrinth, the Minotaur could only be satisfied by feeding on human flesh. Every year, 14 young Athenians were thrown into the maze as a sacrifice to the monster.

The bull-headed Minotaur was kept at the center of a vast labyrinth.

After struggling for hours, Theseus finally throws the ferocious Minotaur to the floor.

A Fight to the Death

Determined to slay the Minotaur, Theseus volunteered to enter the Labyrinth. King Minos's daughter, Ariadne, had fallen in love with Theseus and gave him a ball of golden string to help him find his way out again. As the hero wandered through the dark tunnels, he unraveled the string behind him.

Rounding a corner, Theseus suddenly glimpsed two eyes that burned in the darkness, and then the snarling Minotaur was upon him. Theseus and the monster struggled for many hours until finally the bloodied hero drove his sword through the creature's heart. By following the string, Theseus was able to escape from the Labyrinth and return to Athens.

The goddess Athena with Theseus and the slain Minotaur.

THE TROJAN WAR

Described in Greek myth as the most beautiful woman in the world, Helen was the wife of King Menelaus of Sparta. When she was stolen away by a Trojan prince called Paris, the Greeks united to besiege the city of Troy and bring Helen back. After ten years of war between the Greeks and Trojans, the Greeks finally tricked the Trojans into defeat.

A scene from The Iliad, *Homer's epic poem set during the Trojan War.*

THE WOODEN HORSE

The Greek hero Odysseus came up with the cunning plan to find a way through Troy's city wall. A giant wooden horse was built, and Odysseus and other warriors hid in its hollow belly. The Greek fleet set sail and the Trojans, believing their enemy had finally given up, dragged the "gift horse" into the city.

That night, the Greeks crept out of their hiding place and silently opened the city gates. The fleet returned and Greek warriors poured through the gates to conquer Troy.

ANCIENT ROME

Legend tells of how the great city of Rome was founded by Romulus in 753 BC. At the height of its power, in AD 117, Rome ruled over one of the greatest empires the world has ever seen. It included most of the land around the Mediterranean Sea, and stretched from Britain to the Middle East.

The Rise of Rome

Rome was first ruled by kings. Then, in 509 BC, Rome became a republic governed by a council of wealthy men called the Senate. In 27 BC, Augustus became the first Roman emperor. The last Roman emperor was deposed in AD 476, but the influence of Rome on the world—on languages, architecture, and laws—is still felt today.

The Roman emperor Augustus ruled until his death in AD 14.

The Roman military was the mightiest force in the ancient world.

A Mighty Empire

Rome was built on seven hills near the Tiber River. It had a strong army, which fought for new lands and protected the empire. Cities across the empire were connected by thousands of miles of well-built roads, and the Romans built beautiful temples and baths.

GODS AND GODDESSES

The Romans were heavily influenced by Greek culture. Many of the Roman gods matched the Greek Olympian gods, though almost all were given different names.

ROMAN	GREEK COUNTERPART
JUPITER, KING OF THE GODS	**ZEUS**
JUNO, QUEEN OF THE GODS	**HERA**
NEPTUNE, GOD OF THE SEA	**POSEIDON**
PLUTO, GOD OF THE UNDERWORLD	**HADES**
MINERVA, GODDESS OF KNOWLEDGE	**ATHENA**
APOLLO, GOD OF SUN	**APOLLO**
DIANA, GODDESS OF THE HUNT	**ARTEMIS**
MARS, GOD OF WAR	**ARES**
MERCURY, GOD OF TRADE	**HERMES**
CERES, GODDESS OF FARMING	**DEMETER**
VESTA, GODDESS OF THE HEARTH	**HESTIA**
VENUS, GODDESS OF LOVE	**APHRODITE**

AENEAS

The greatest hero of Roman myth was Aeneas, the son of the goddess Venus and a prince called Anchises. When the Greeks sacked Troy, Aeneas fought bravely on until the end. Ordered to flee by the gods, the hero escaped the city's burning ruins, carrying his father on his back.

Aeneas and Dido

Aeneas and a band of other Trojan survivors wandered the seas for six years. Eventually, their vessel was shipwrecked on the African coast at Carthage, where Queen Dido welcomed them. Aeneas and Dido fell in love, but the gods feared that Aeneas would be distracted from his destiny. The god Mercury ordered Aeneas to leave Carthage, and the hero reluctantly abandoned Dido and set sail. Mad with grief, the queen fell upon a sword and killed herself.

A Roman mosaic from the fourth century showing Dido and Aeneas.

Journey to the Underworld

In a dream, Aeneas's dead father summoned his son to the underworld. A priestess, the Sybil, was Aeneas's guide on the dangerous journey. Once in the field of spirits, the hero saw the souls of his dead war comrades and that of his former love, Dido. He tried to excuse his previous behavior, but Dido turned her face away from him. Later Aeneas was greeted by his father, who foretold his son's future triumphs and the eventual founding of Rome.

The warrior Aeneas appears in both Greek and Roman mythology.

BECOMING A GOD

Once in Italy, Aeneas sided with King Latinus and was betrothed to his daughter, Lavinia. Enraged by jealousy, Lavinia's former suitor, Turnus, declared war against the Trojan. After a period of bloody fighting, Aeneas killed Turnus and went on to found the city of Lavinium. After Aeneas's death, Venus asked Jupiter to make her son immortal, and the hero was raised up as the god Jupiter Indiges.

Aeneas killed the prince-warrior Turnus with his sword.

ROMULUS AND REMUS

The twin brothers Romulus and Remus were the sons of the god Mars and a princess called Rhea Silver. She was the daughter of King Numitor of Alba Longa, who had been overthrown by his jealous brother, Amulius. When the twins were born, Amulius feared that they would one day seek to reclaim the kingdom, and so he threw both boys and their mother into the Tiber River.

Amulius throws the twins into the river in this German painting.

The baby twins were raised by a she-wolf.

The Founding of Rome

Rhea Silver drowned, but the twins were eventually swept ashore. There, they were discovered by a she-wolf, who suckled them as if they were her cubs. One day, a shepherd called Faustulus discovered the boys running wild in the woods. He had once worked for King Numitor and realized who the children were. Taking them home, Faustulus raised the twins as his own sons. When they were old enough, he revealed their true identity to them.

Together, Romulus and Remus killed their wicked uncle Amulius and released their grandfather. They then began building a city on the Tiber at the place where they had been washed ashore. However, they argued over who would be the city's king. Romulus killed his brother and named the city "Rome," after himself.

A Roman altar showing the founding of Rome.

Romulus, Remus, and the she-wolf on a 16th-century coin.

THE VIKINGS

During the age of the Vikings, seaborne warriors spread terror across Europe. The legends of these Norse people tell of how the mighty world tree, Yggdrasil, was created at the beginning of time. In its different realms lived many fantastic beings from powerful gods to horrifying monsters.

Land of Warriors and Seafarers

34

Vikings tore through villages looting and killing at will with swords and axes.

From the eighth to the eleventh centuries, Viking warriors from Norway, Sweden, and Denmark spread terror across Europe as they raided foreign lands for precious treasures and to seize new land. The Vikings were wonderful storytellers, and their thrilling tales of battles, gods, and terrifying monsters, live on in legends.

Fierce Warriors

The Vikings were great sailors, traders, and craftsmen, but they are mainly remembered as fierce warriors. They launched lightning-swift attacks all around the coasts of Europe. The "beserkers" were the most feared of all Viking warriors. Working themselves into a frenzied rage before battle, they terrified their victims by howling like beasts and biting their shields.

Discovering New Lands

The Vikings left the safety of their shores to travel thousands of miles in search of new lands. As they braved the icy waters of the North Atlantic, many ships were lost in storms, but that didn't stop the Vikings from reaching Iceland, Greenland, and eventually Newfoundland in North America.

A reconstruction of a Viking house in Newfoundland.

Masters of the Sea

The Vikings built many kinds of ships, but most famous are the long "dragonboats" that swiftly carried warriors across the sea. It is not known how the Vikings crossed thousands of miles of stormy waters without charts or compasses. They would have relied on the sun, stars, and moon to calculate their position, and they must have had a good knowledge of wind and wave patterns and sea life.

The Oseberg ship was found in a burial mound in Norway.

This Swedish rune stone shows a Viking warship.

Runes

Although the Vikings did not leave behind any written documents, letters called "runes" carved on stone or wood provide clues about their traditions. Glorious battles and heroic warriors were celebrated on memorial stones called "rune stones."

The Viking Universe

The Vikings believed that the universe was ruled over by many gods and goddesses, and that amazing creatures lived in its various parts. At the center of the universe was Yggdrasil, an immense ash tree that held everything together.

Tree of Life

With its branches stretching up into the heavens, Yggdrasil connected the various kingdoms of Norse mythology. Humans lived in Midgard, which was surrounded by an ocean containing a giant serpent. The gods were found in Asgard and Vanaheim, while giants, trolls, and other fantastic beings lived in separate kingdoms. At the bottom of the tree was Niflheim, an icy place of eternal darkness.

Vanaheim, the world of the "Vanir" gods

Bifrost, the burning rainbow bridge connecting Midgard and Asgard

Svartalfheim, the land of the dark elves

Nidavellir, the land of the dwarfs

Muspell, the world of fire

Chief Gods

Asgard, the world of the most important "Aesir" gods

Valhalla, the majestic hall ruled over by the god Odin

Alfheim, the land of the light elves

Midgard, or Earth, the realm of human beings

Jotunheim, the land of the giants

Niflheim, the icy underworld of the dead

Odin was the god of war and wisdom, whose one eye was said to blaze like the sun. Odin's son, Thor, was the god of thunder. He was incredibly strong, though not as clever as Odin. Eager to take on any challenge, Thor once held a drinking contest with giants and swallowed so much sea that the tide went out. Freyr was the god of fertility and birth.

Thor's hammer pendant. I can imagine it hanging around a Viking warrior's neck. Did he feel certain Thor would watch over him?

Stella Caldwell

A Valkyrie flies across the battlefield.

VALHALLA

In Norse legends, female warriors called Valkyries flew over the battlefields, gathering up the souls of the dead and carrying them to Valhalla, a majestic banquet hall located in Asgard and ruled over by Odin. Here, slain warriors feasted and prepared for "Ragnarök," the great battle that would take place between the gods and the forces of evil at the end of the world.

ODÍN

Known as the "Allfather," Odin was the one-eyed god of war, wisdom, magic, and poetry. Together with his two brothers, Vili and Ve, Odin created the Earth, and the first man and woman. Incredibly powerful, Odin could cause war on Earth simply by throwing his spear.

Quest for Wisdom

Legend tells that Odin longed to discover the secret of the runes that were carved into the trunk of Yggdrasil. These runes were said to contain the destiny of everything. In order to gain this knowledge, Odin hung himself from a branch, pierced by his own spear, for nine days.

On another occasion, Odin asked the giant Mimir for a drink from the well of knowledge. Mimir agreed on one condition: that Odin gave an eye in return. Odin was prepared to pay this price for wisdom, and so he gouged out one eye and dropped it into the well.

Odin was the chief of the Norse gods.

Ravens and Wolves

Odin had two ravens, Huginn and Muninn, upon which he bestowed the gift of speech. Each day at dawn, the god sent the birds out to fly around the world. Returning in the evening, the ravens perched on Odin's shoulders and kept him informed of what they had seen and heard. Odin's other companions were a pair of wolves called Geri and Freki, which he fed from his own table.

Odin and his companions: two ravens and two wolves.

A Mighty Steed

Odin rode between the kingdoms of Yggdrasil on his eight-legged horse, Sleipnir. This magical steed was the son of the shapeshifting god Loki, who gave birth in the form of a mare, and a stallion belonging to a giant.

This Swedish rune stone shows Sleipnir carrying Odin.

Thor's Hammer

One famous saga, or long Viking story, is about Thor's magic hammer. The mighty god Thor awoke one day to discover that his powerful hammer, Mjölnir, had been stolen. The thief was Thrym, king of the giants.

A Cunning Plan

Thrym revealed that he would only return the hammer to Thor if the beautiful goddess Freya married him. So the gods hatched a plan–Thor would dress as Freya with the trickster god Loki disguised as her bridesmaid. The two then set off to Thrym's castle for a feast.

Thor almost gave himself away by consuming an entire ox, but Loki assured Thrym that Freya was just hungry. When the giant lifted his bride's veil to kiss her, he was alarmed at her burning eyes. However, Loki told Thrym that Freya was merely tired. As the giant fetched the magic hammer to bless the marriage, Thor seized his prized weapon and beat Thrym to death.

Thor beating the giant to death, while Loki is disguised as a bridesmaid.

*Thor's powerful
hammer, Mjölnir.*

At Ragnarök, Thor would fight the Midgard serpent.

THE DOOM OF THE GODS

Ragnarök was the epic battle that would take place between the gods and forces of evil at the end of the world. Ragnarök means "the doom of the gods." It was believed that the wolf Fenrir would devour the sun and moon, and stars would tumble from the sky. Surt, leader of the fire giants, would set the world ablaze, and only Odin's son, Vidar, and one human couple would survive. When the battle was over, these two humans would be the first people of the new world.

The Giants

The Norse giants were frequently at war with the gods. They were known as the *jötnar* or the "devourers" and their home was the realm of Jotunheim, a place of mountains, deep forests, and wilderness.

The Frost Giant

Formed at the beginning of time, Ymir was an evil frost giant who emerged from rivers of ice. As he slept, many other giants were formed from his sweat. They fed on the milk of an enormous cow that licked the ice as if it were grass. From the ice, the first god, Buri, appeared–he was the grandfather of the gods Odin, Vili, and Ve.

Odin and his brothers killed Ymir, and as the giant's blood gushed from his body, it drowned all the other giants except for Bergelmir and his wife. They escaped and founded a new race of frost giants.

The Norse giants came from Jotunheim, an icy wilderness.

The Creation

Once Ymir was dead, Odin and his brothers used the giant's body to form the world. They made the earth from his flesh and mountains from his bones. His teeth were turned into stones and his blood into seas. Then the gods created the sky from Ymir's great skull and turned the giant's eyebrows into a huge wall to protect the human world of Midgard.

At the beginning of time, Ymir emerged from rivers of ice.

STONE AND FIRE GIANTS

Although a few giants, such as the mountain giantess Skaldi, were good-looking and good-natured, many others were spiteful and hideously ugly. Hrungnir, the mightiest of all the giants, had a head and heart made of stone–he was killed in a duel with the god Thor. The Vikings believed that the fire giants would engulf the world in flames at the final battle of Ragnarök.

The giant Hrungnir is overcome by the god Thor in a duel.

FROST GIANTS

The evil frost giants lived in the icy, mountainous wilderness known as Jotunheim. Hideous, hulking, and extraordinarily strong, they were often in conflict with the gods.

THE DWARFS

Deep underground, in a complex of caves and tunnels called Nidavellir, lived the dwarfs. They were master craftsmen, skilled in working gold, silver, and gems. The dwarfs avoided daylight at all costs, for the sun's rays turned them to stone.

A dwarf creating Fenrir's unbreakable chain.

A stunning brooch inlaid with precious stones from Norway.

Magical Treasures

Known for their wisdom and magical powers, the dwarfs crafted many treasures. These included Mjölnir, Thor's magical hammer and Gleipnir, the unbreakable chain that bound the ferocious wolf Fenrir. Skidbladnir–"the best of ships"–could sail on any sea and was large enough to hold all the gods. When it wasn't needed, the ship could magically fold up to fit inside a pocket.

Skidbladnir sailed on water, in the air, and over land.

A Viking mount to put a horse's bridle on, covered in gold leaf.

This 10th-century forge stone discovered on a Danish beach shows Loki with his lips sewn together.

Loki's Bet

The trickster god Loki once bet his head that the treasures crafted by the dwarf sons of Ivaldi–including Odin's magical spear–could not be bettered. The dwarf Brokk took up the challenge, and he and his brother Eitri set to work on a magical hammer. Loki transformed himself into a fly to distract the pair as they worked, but Brokk still won the bet.

When the dwarfs came to claim Loki's head, he said they were welcome to it but had no right to any part of his neck. Since neither side could decide where the head ended and the neck began, Loki was instead punished by having his mouth sewn shut.

Mighty Monsters

Loki and the giantess Angrboda had three monstrous children. They were the ferocious wolf Fenrir, the massive serpent Jormungand, and Hel, who was half-alive and half-dead. The gods captured all three and brought them to Asgard. The serpent was thrown into the ocean, Hel into the icy underworld of Niflheim, and Fenrir was kept in Asgard.

The Vikings believed that Fenrir would break free of his chains at the battle of Ragnarök.

The god Tyr binding Fenrir with the unbreakable chain.

Bound in Chains

As the wolf pup Fenrir grew, the gods became alarmed by his incredible strength. Thinking they could trick him, they told Fenrir he was weak and challenged him to prove otherwise. Fenrir agreed to be bound in iron chains but he easily broke free. So the gods asked the dwarfs to create a magical chain that would restrain the wolf forever.

Fenrír Bítes Back

When this chain was complete, the gods once again questioned Fenrir's strength. Fenrir suspected treachery, and he agreed to be bound only if the god Tyr placed his hand in his jaws. Tyr reluctantly agreed, and when Fenrir discovered he was unable to break free, he ripped Tyr's hand from his arm.

HEL

Hel was the goddess of death and the underworld.

In the dark realm of Niflheim, Hel ruled over the dead. Only glorious warriors sent to Valhalla, the hall of the slain, escaped her clutches. The wicked were tortured in a castle filled with the venom of snakes.

THE MIDGARD SERPENT

After Odin tossed Jormungand into the ocean, the serpent grew so enormous that he completely encircled the Earth. Even the gods were terrified of him, for this dreadful monster could rise up from the water to crush his victims with massive coils or kill them with deadly venom. Jormungand's archenemy was the god Thor. It was said that at the last battle of Ragnarök, the two were destined to slay one another.

Sigurd and the Dragon

K ing Sigmund was a legendary warrior who was killed in battle. His sword, which was shattered during the fight, had been a gift from the god Odin. Searching the battlefield after the king's death, his wife gathered up the pieces of the magical sword and treasured them.

A Dragon's Hoard

Sigmund's son, Sigurd, longed for a life of adventure. His tutor was a blacksmith named Regin, whose brother had been killed by Odin. Odin had given Regin's father a hoard of treasure in compensation. These riches should have been inherited by Regin, but a dragon called Fafnir had stolen them. Regin told Sigurd that if he killed the dragon and brought back the treasure, he would share it with him.

SLAYING THE BEAST

Sigurd's mother gave her son the fragments of his father's sword. Regin used them to forge a sword so sharp that it could slice through iron. Armed with this fearsome weapon, known as Gram, Sigurd set off to kill the dragon. He soon found the beast's lair and hid in a shallow pit. After a while, Fafnir lumbered over the pit and Sigurd drove his sword into the dragon's heart.

This 12th-century carving of the fight is from Hylestad, Norway.

Sigurd killing Fafnir with the sword called Gram.

Some of the dead beast's blood dripped onto Sigurd's lips, and suddenly he found he could understand what the birds in the trees were saying. They shrieked of how Regin was plotting to kill him and take all the treasure for himself. Sigurd then realized that he had no choice but to slay Regin, too.

THE ANCIENT EGYPTIANS

The myths of ancient Egypt tell of how the world emerged from a vast, dark sea. The Egyptian gods ruled over every aspect of life, and were worshipped in sacred temple rituals. People feared the spirits that stalked the land of the living, and the dreadful monsters that lay in wait in the dark underworld.

LAND OF GODS AND MAGIC

Around 5,000 years ago, the ancient Egyptians established a civilization that would last for over 3,000 years. It was a land rich in magic and mystery and had few equals in the beauty of its art or monuments.

God-Kings

Egypt was first united under one ruler called Narmer, around 3000 BC. A succession of pharaohs ruled over the land until the death of the last one, Cleopatra, in 30 BC. Egyptian pharaohs were believed to be "god-kings," filled with the power of the god Horus. Some pharaohs were buried inside huge stone pyramids. Later pharaohs were buried in rock-cut tombs in the Valley of the Kings.

This ancient siltstone palette depicts the unification of Egypt by King Narmer.

Kingdom of the Nile

Without the Nile River, there could have been no great civilization in Egypt. Each summer the Nile flooded, leaving behind a black mud that fertilized the land and made it an ideal place to farm. The Egyptians called their country "Kemet," or the Black Land. On either side was a vast desert known as "Deshret," or the Red Land.

The Egyptians built magnificent temples and palaces along the Nile River.

Picture Writing

Egyptian writing is made up of around 700 symbols called hieroglyphs. It was used to write on papyrus scrolls, and to inscribe temples and tombs. Over the years, the skill of reading hieroglyphs was gradually lost. However, in 1822, Jean-Francois Champollion was able to decipher the hieroglyphs inscribed on the Rosetta Stone (which had been discovered in 1799). It is thanks to his work that we know much about ancient Egypt.

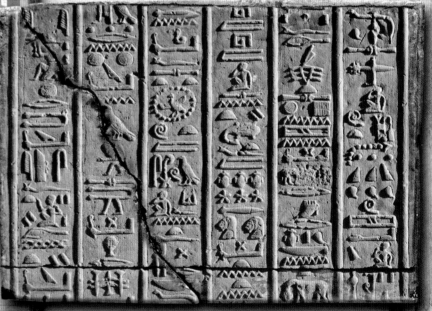

Heiroglyphs inscribed on the walls of the Temple of Kom Ombo in Egypt.

Gods and Religion

The ancient Egyptians worshipped over 2,000 gods and goddesses. Some, like the sun god Ra, were important across Egypt. Others, such as the cat goddess Bastet, were only worshipped in certain areas.

Bastet was the goddess of fire, cats, and the home.

Gods and Goddesses

Most Egyptian gods represented a particular aspect of the world. Osiris was the god of the dead, while Anubis was the god of embalming, and Thoth was the god of wisdom. Many gods were associated with an animal and were depicted in more than one way. For example, Hathor, the goddess of motherhood, is shown as a cow or as a woman, or as a combination of the two.

Ra

Osiris

Isis

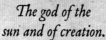

The god of the sun and of creation.

The god of the dead and the underworld.

The wife of Osiris and the goddess of fertility.

Houses for the Gods

The magnificent temples that stood along the banks of the Nile were built as dwelling places for the gods. Only pharaohs and priests were allowed to worship in them. Ordinary people could pray outside the temples, or worship at the shrines of lesser gods.

Mummies and Coffins

The ancient Egyptians believed that as long as a dead body was preserved, then a person's soul could live forever in the afterlife. Mummification involved a process that took 70 days. After a dead person's organs had been removed (apart from the precious heart), the body was dried out and wrapped in bandages. The mummy was placed inside a coffin. A rich person might have several beautifully decorated coffins, one inside another.

Egyptians mummified their dead in preparation for the afterlife.

Horus

God of the sky. His spirit entered Egypt's pharaohs.

Anubis

The god of embalming and funeral rites.

Thoth

The god of wisdom and the patron of scribes.

Seth

Osiris's brother and the god of darkness and chaos.

Journey to the Afterlife

The ancient Egyptians believed that beneath Earth was a vast underworld called Duat. It was filled with perils and hideous monsters, and so the journey to the afterlife– "the field of reeds"–was fraught with danger.

The Book of the Dead

Magic spells were often written on papyrus scrolls, coffins, or tomb walls. These texts, now known as *The Book of the Dead*, held the key to surviving the dangers of the underworld.

The most important test came in the Hall of Two Truths. Here, a person's heart was weighed against the feather of Ma'at, the goddess of truth. If the person had not led a good life and the heart was judged to be too heavy, then Ammit, "Devourer of the Dead," consumed it and the soul was refused entry to the afterlife.

In The Book of the Dead, Ammit (far right) stands ready to devour a heart.

A priest performs the opening-of-the-mouth ritual on Pharaoh Tutankhamun's mummy.

The Opening of the Mouth Ceremony

This important ritual allowed the senses of a dead person to be "freed" so they could be useful in the afterlife. At the door of the tomb, the mummy was placed in an upright position and a priest used sacred tools to touch its face.

This tomb painting shows a deceased couple (left) worshipping the gods of Duat.

Model Servants

Ancient Egyptians worried that they might be expected to work in the afterlife. Wealthy people were often buried with small "shabti" figures. It was thought that these model servants, inscribed with a magic spell, would be able to perform the tasks instead.

Ammit, Devourer of the Dead

In the dark realms of the underworld, Ammit waited to devour the hearts of those who were judged to have led a wicked life. With the head of a crocodile, the torso of a lion, and the hindquarters of a hippopotamus, this demon of destruction was made up of the most ferocious animals known to the ancient Egyptians.

Osiris and Isis

From Geb, the sky god, and Nut, the goddess of the Earth, came the children Osiris, Isis, Seth, and Nephthys. Osiris became king of Egypt and married his sister, Isis. Osiris was a good ruler and much loved. Only Seth was unhappy, because he was jealous and longed to be king himself.

The Evil Seth

Seth invited Osiris to a banquet and placed a large coffin, decorated with precious stones, in the center of the room. Seth told his guests it would be a prize for the person who fitted the chest best.

One by one, the guests tried it out, but when Osiris climbed in, Seth slammed down the lid and locked it. The coffin was thrown into the Nile, and the river carried Osiris's body far out to sea.

The evil Seth tricks his brother, Osiris, into climbing into the chest.

The First Mummy

Isis was heartbroken and swore she would find her husband again. Wandering the world, she at last found the coffin magically entwined in the trunk of a tamarisk tree and brought it back to Egypt. However, Seth discovered her secret and hacked Osiris's body into pieces, scattering them along the Nile.

Now Isis transformed herself into a bird of prey and found all but one of the body parts. With the help of the god Anubis, she wrapped them in cloth and laid them out in the shape of Osiris. Isis then kissed the mummy, and Osiris was reborn as lord of the underworld.

God of the Sky

After Isis had pieced Osiris's body back together again, she became pregnant. To escape Seth, she fled to the Nile Delta marshlands, where she bore her divine son, Horus. He was said to be the sky itself, and his right eye was the sun and his left eye the moon.

Horus's divine spirit was believed to enter Egypt's pharaohs.

Ra, the Sun God

K ing of the gods, the sun god Ra was the bringer of light and the giver of life. Some myths told of how, at the beginning of time, there was nothing but a dark ocean called Nun. From out of these waters emerged Ra. With his breath and saliva, Ra created Shu (air) and Tefnut (moisture), and from this divine pair emerged the sky goddess Nut and earth god Geb.

Ra on his sun boat during his daily journey across the sky.

Dangerous Journey

Every day Ra sailed across the heavens in a sun-boat called "the boat of a million years." At the end of the day, Ra sank below the horizon to face the powers of darkness. Traveling through the dangerous realms of the underworld in another solar boat, Ra had to battle the serpent-demon known as Apophis. After defeating this monster, Ra would rise triumphant in the east and the sun would once again shine over Egypt.

Ra was the god of the sun and also of creation.

The Eye of Ra

In one myth, Ra became angry with mankind because humans were not following his laws. As a punishment, he sent the lioness-headed goddess Sekhmet to strike terror in the hearts of men. However, once Sekhmet had started slaughtering people, she grew more and more bloodthirsty. Ra realized that Sekhmet would destroy the human race if she was not stopped.

He ordered his servants to brew 7,000 jars of beer and colour it red. The mixture was poured over some fields and when Sekhmet saw it she immediately began to drink the "blood." The goddess became drunk and fell into asleep for several days. When she awoke, her thirst for blood had disappeared.

This sculpture of Sekhmet was discovered in the tomb of Pharaoh Tutankhamun.

"Hail to thee, Ra, master of Ma'at, who sits in the chapel, master of the gods!"

From *The Book of the Dead*

Demons and Sorcery

In Egyptian myths, magic–called *heka*–was a powerful force that existed before the world was created. In the underworld, demons threatened dead souls as they tried to reach the afterlife, and even the mighty Ra was not safe from the monster Apophis. In the land of the living, demons and evil spirits were blamed for people's misfortunes.

A pendant amulet depicting a vulture, made with gold and lapis lazuli.

Magic Spells

The temple gods played little part in everyday life, and in times of illness or crisis, Egyptians turned to magic. Priests were the guardians of this secret knowledge. Spells were used for healing, to guard against dangers, and to ward off troublesome ghosts of the dead. They could also be used to activate protective charms called amulets as well as magical potions.

Demon of Darkness

Apophis, the "eater of souls," was an enormous serpent that dwelled in the underworld. This serpent was considered to be all-powerful, and could never be destroyed, only briefly defeated. Occasionally Apophis overcame Ra in their nightly battles. The ancient Egyptians believed that violent storms or a terrifying solar eclipse were the result.

The sun god fighting Apophis during their nightly battle.

The Eye of Horus

Charms and amulets were worn to protect both the living and dead from harm. The eyes of the falcon-headed god Horus were said to be the sun and the moon, and so the "Eye of Horus" became a particularly powerful amulet.

The Eye of Horus. How much trust the peoples of ancient Egypt must have placed in this ultimate symbol of protection!

Stella Caldwell

MAGICAL CREATURES

Egyptian mythology is full of fantastic beings and creatures. The gods were often depicted as half human and half animal. Many other strange creatures, such as serpent-necked leopards or winged griffins (part lion, part eagle), are depicted in Egyptian art.

The Great Sphinx

Standing solemn and silent in the Egyptian desert, a strange beast with the head of a pharaoh and the body of a lion stares out towards the rising sun. Between its paws is the dream stele of the pharaoh Thutmose IV. It tells of how, as a young prince, Thutmose was out hunting when he fell asleep in the shadow of the Sphinx's head (which at that time was almost completely buried in sand.)

The giant Sphinx still lies near the pyramids at Giza in Egypt.

Thutmose's Dream

Thutmose dreamed that the sun god told him he would be king of all Egypt if he cleared the sand away from the monument. When Thutmose awoke, he did as he had been instructed, and eventually became pharaoh.

The Bennu Bird

The Egyptians believed that the Bennu Bird was connected to the sun god Ra and to creation and rebirth. Like the magical firebird, the phoenix, it was believed to be self-created. Some myths told of how the Bennu Bird rose from the flames that burned on the sacred Persea tree in the ancient city of Heliopolis.

The Bennu Bird was a symbol of rebirth in ancient Egypt.

ACKNOWLEDGEMENTS

In my career as an archaeologist I have made many compelling finds. However, it would never have occurred to me to write a book on the subject of gods and monsters had it not been for the strange events outlined in my introduction.

The wonderful artifacts displayed in these pages from different worlds and cultures showed me that the gods, heroes, and monsters of ancient mythologies share many intriguing similarities.

In drawing upon that inspiration, I have been helped by many and I would like to thank the following individuals for their help in compiling this book: my editor, Selina Wood; Jake da'Costa and WildPixel Ltd, for design and CGI artworks; Leo Brown, for pencil artworks; Steve Behan, for picture research; and Charlotte Larcombe, for production.

Stella Caldwell

The publishers would like to thank the following sources for their kind permission to reproduce the pictures in this book.

5t. Werner Forman/Universal Images Group/Getty Images, 5b. Royal Armouries Museum, 6-7. Anax/Bloomberg via Getty Images, 8l. Private Collection, 8c. Bridgeman Images, 9. Shutterstock.com, 28, akg-images/Erich Lessing, 12. & 13. Shutterstock.com, 16l. Shutterstock.com, 17t. Fine Art Images/Heritage Images/Getty Images, 17b. Shutterstock.com, 19t. DEA/G. Dagli Orti/De Agostini/Getty Images, 19b. CM Dixon/Print Collector/Getty Images, 20 Hulton Archive/Getty Images, 22. Mimmo Jodice/Corbis, 23. Museo Arqueologico Nacional, Madrid, Spain/Bridgeman Images, 24. Getty Images, 26. CM Dixon/Print Collector/Getty Images, 26-27. AKG-Images/Peter Connolly, 27. DeAgostini/Getty Images, 28. Somerset County Museum, Taunton Castle, UK/Bridgeman Images, 29. DEA/G. Nimatallah/Getty Images, 30br. Private Collection, 30-31. Leeds Museums and Art Galleries/Bridgeman Images, 31b & 31br. DEA/A. Dagli Orti/De Agostini/Getty Images, 35tr. Yves Marcoux/First Light/Corbis, 35r. Werner Forman/Universal Images Group/Getty Images, 35bl. The Art Archive, 37c. Werner Forman/Universal Images Group/Getty Images, 37t. Getty Images, 39t. Private Collection/© Look and Learn/Bridgeman Images, 39b. CM Dixon/Print Collector/Getty Images, 41r. Chronicle/Alamy Stock Photo, 42. & 63c. Istockphoto.com, 43br Private Collection, 46l. & 46-47b Werner Forman/Corbis, 47t. & 48bl. Werner Forman/Universal Images Group/Getty Images, 49c. Istockphoto.com, 53r. DeAgostini/Getty Images, 54c. Istockphoto.com, 54b. Shutterstock.com, 56. Werner Forman Archive, 56-57. Istockphoto.com, 57r. Stuart Dee/Getty Images, 58l. Louvre, Paris, France/Peter Willi/Bridgeman Images, 58-59. Shutterstock.com, 59r. akg-images/De Agostini Picture Lib./S. Vannini, 60b. British Museum, London, UK/Bridgeman Images, 60-61. DeAgostini/Getty Images, 61t. Valley of the Kings, Thebes, Egypt/Bridgeman Images, 61b. Art Media/Print Collector/Getty Images, 64l. Mary Evans Picture Library, 64-65. akg-images/Tristan Lafranchis, 65. Shutterstock.com, 66l. akg/North Wind Picture Archives, 67r. Werner Forman/Corbis, 68. Egyptian National Museum, Cairo, Egypt/Photo © Boltin Picture Library/Bridgeman Images, 70-71. © Universal Images Group/DeAgostini/Alamy Stock Photo, 69. Shutterstock.com, 71. Ancient Art & Architecture Collection Ltd/Alamy Stock Photo, 71br.

Every effort has been made to acknowledge correctly and contact the source and/or copyright holder of each picture and Carlton Books Limited apologises for any unintentional errors or omissions that will be corrected in future editions of this book.

THIS IS A CARLTON BOOK
Text, design, and illustration © Carlton Books Limited 2016
Published in 2016 by Carlton Books Limited
An imprint of the Carlton Publishing Group
20 Mortimer Street, London W1T 3JW.

ISBN: 978-1-78312-191-5
Printed in China.